Dear Parents and Educators,

Welcome to Penguin Young Readers! As parents and educators, you know that each child develops at his or her own pace—in terms of speech, critical thinking, and, of course, reading. Penguin Young Readers recognizes this fact. As a result, each Penguin Young Readers book is assigned a traditional easy-to-read level (1–4) as well as a Guided Reading Level (A–P). Both of these systems will help you choose the right book for your child. Please refer to the back of each book for specific leveling information. Penguin Young Readers features esteemed authors and illustrators, stories about favorite characters, fascinating nonfiction, and more!

Ham-Ham-Hamsters

LEVEL **2**

GUIDED
READING
LEVEL **I**

This book is perfect for a **Progressing Reader** who:
- can figure out unknown words by using picture and context clues;
- can recognize beginning, middle, and ending sounds;
- can make and confirm predictions about what will happen in the text; and
- can distinguish between fiction and nonfiction.

Here are some **activities** you can do during and after reading this book:
- Nonfiction: Nonfiction books deal with facts and events that are real. Talk about the elements of nonfiction. On a separate sheet of paper, write down what you learned about hamsters.
- Make Connections: In this book, you learned how to take good care of a hamster. If you had one, how would you take care of it? If you do have a hamster, what do you think is the most important part of caring for it?

Remember, sharing the love of reading with a child is the best gift you can give!

—Sarah Fabiny, Editorial Director
  Penguin Young Readers program

*Penguin Young Readers are leveled by independent reviewers applying the standards developed by Irene Fountas and Gay Su Pinnell in *Matching Books to Readers: Using Leveled Books in Guided Reading*, Heinemann, 1999.

For all the students and teachers who care
for their pet hamsters—BB

PENGUIN YOUNG READERS
An Imprint of Penguin Random House LLC

Penguin supports copyright. Copyright fuels creativity, encourages diverse voices,
promotes free speech, and creates a vibrant culture. Thank you for buying an authorized edition
of this book and for complying with copyright laws by not reproducing, scanning, or distributing
any part of it in any form without permission. You are supporting writers and allowing Penguin
to continue to publish books for every reader.

Photo credits: cover, page 3: © Thinkstock/karlbarrett; page 4: © Thinkstock/Jeffrey Van daele;
page 5: © Thinkstock/karlbarrett; page 6: (top) © Thinkstock/s-a-m, (middle, bottom) © Thinkstock/
IgorKovalchuk; page 7: (top) © Thinkstock/IgorKovalchuk, (middle) © Thinkstock/GlobalP,
(bottom) © Thinkstock/lepas2004; page 8: (mouse) © Thinkstock/CreativeNature_nl,
(rat) © Thinkstock/Pakhnyushchyy, (squirrel) © Thinkstock/irin717; page 9: © Thinkstock/
wolfhound911; page 10–11: © Superstock/imageBROKER; page 12: © Superstock/age footstock;
page 13: © Superstock/Biosphoto; page 14: © Superstock/M. Watson; page 15: © Superstock/
M. Watson; page 16–17: © Superstock/age fotostock; page 18: © Thinkstock/victoriarak;
page 19: (big hamster) © Thinkstock/GlobalP, (ruler) © Thinkstock/Devonyu; page 20: © Thinkstock/
andylid; page 21: (hamsters) © Thinkstock/RuslanOmega, (cage) © Thinkstock/9george;
page 22: © Thinkstock/YouraPechkin; page 23: (top) © Thinkstock/Martina_L, (middle) Thinkstock/
GlobalP, (bottom) Thinkstock/s-a-m; page 24: © Thinkstock/mu_mu_; page 25: © Superstock/NaturePL;
page 26: © Thinkstock/atosf; page 27: © Thinkstock/shawn_ang; page 28: © Thinkstock/EBlokhina;
page 29: © Thinkstock/CassiekTait; page 30–31: © Thinkstock/Khmel; page 32: © Getty/FRANCK FIFE.

Text copyright © 2016 by Bonnie Bader. All rights reserved. Published by Penguin Young Readers,
an imprint of Penguin Random House LLC, 345 Hudson Street, New York, New York 10014.
Manufactured in China.

Library of Congress Cataloging-in-Publication Data is available.

ISBN 9780399541650 (pbk)   10 9 8 7 6 5 4 3 2 1
ISBN 9780399541667 (hc)   10 9 8 7 6 5 4 3 2 1

Ham-Ham-Hamsters

by Bonnie Bader

Penguin Young Readers
An Imprint of Penguin Random House

Ham.

Ham.

Hamsters!

Hamsters are rodents.

Mice, squirrels, and rats

are rodents, too.

Hamsters have soft fur.

They have short tails

and short legs.

They have small ears

and big eyes.

Many hamsters live in the wild.

Dig, dig, dig.

Hamsters live underground.

Their homes are burrows.

A hamster stays in its burrow
all day.
It goes out to look for food
at night.

Sniff, sniff, sniff.

This hamster looks for food.

It cannot see very well.

It uses its nose to find

something to eat.

Hamsters eat seeds, fruits,

and vegetables.

They eat small bugs, too.

Stuff, stuff, stuff.

Hamsters stuff their cheeks

with lots of food.

A hamster can make a good pet.

A hamster can grow to six inches.

Hamsters can be tiny.

Some are between

1½ and 4 inches.

These tiny hamsters can stay

together in a big cage.

21

A wire cage is a good home

for a hamster.

The cage should be strong.

You do not want your hamster

to get out!

If you want a hamster
as a pet, ask an adult.
What kind of hamster would you
want to get?

Put soft paper on the bottom
of the cage.

Hamsters like to make nests.

You can get hamster food

at the pet store.

Hamsters like apples

and carrots, too.

Your hamster will drink water

every day.

Be careful when you pick up
your hamster.

Be careful when you pet it.

Hamsters like to hide.

Hamster, hamster,

where are you?

Run, run, run.

Hamsters like to play

on a wheel

inside the cage.

Hamsters are cute.

Hamsters are tiny.

Hamsters make great pets!